DISNEP
FROZEN II

MUSIC FROM THE MOTION PICTURE SOUNDTRACK

ISBN 978-1-5400-8370-8

Disney Characters and Artwork © 2019 Disney

HAL•LEONARD®

Visit Hal Leonard Online at
www.halleonard.com

Contact us:
Hal Leonard
7777 West Bluemound Road
Milwaukee, WI 53213
Email: info@halleonard.com

In Europe, contact:
Hal Leonard Europe Limited
42 Wigmore Street
Marylebone, London, W1U 2RN
Email: info@halleonardeurope.com

In Australia, contact:
Hal Leonard Australia Pty. Ltd.
4 Lentara Court
Cheltenham, Victoria, 3192 Australia
Email: info@halleonard.com.au

ALL IS FOUND

Music and Lyrics by KRISTEN ANDERSON-LOPEZ
and ROBERT LOPEZ

Where the North-wind meets the sea, there's a riv-er full of mem-o-ry. Sleep, my

dar-ling, safe and sound, for in this riv-er, all is found.

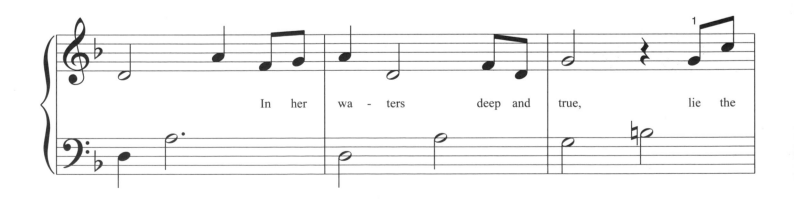

In her wa-ters deep and true, lie the

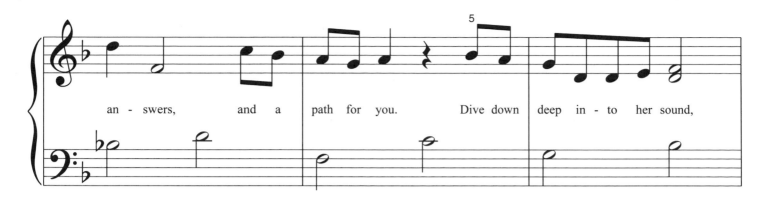

an - swers, and a path for you. Dive down deep in - to her sound,

but not too far, or you'll be drowned. Yes,

she will sing to those who hear; _____ and in her song, _____ all mag - ic

flows. _____ But can you brave what you most fear? Can you

4

face what the riv-er knows. Where the North-wind meets the

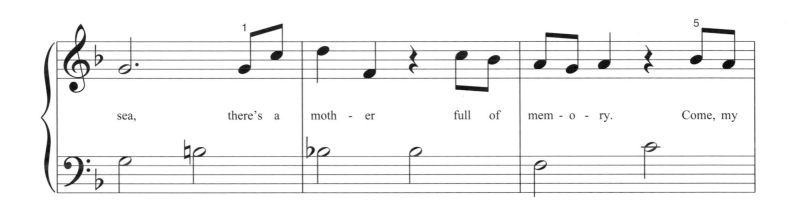

sea, there's a moth-er full of mem-o-ry. Come, my

dar-ling, home-ward bound: when all is lost, then all is found.

SOME THINGS NEVER CHANGE

Music and Lyrics by KRISTEN ANDERSON-LOPEZ
and ROBERT LOPEZ

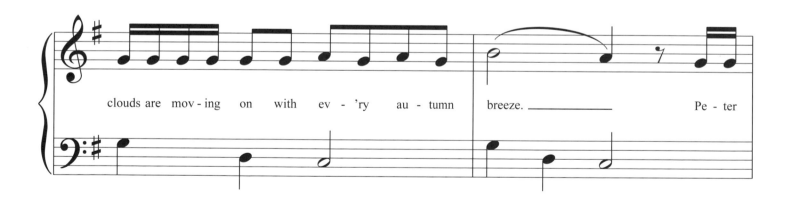

I re - ly on cer - tain cer - tain - ties. Yes,

some things nev - er change, __ like the feel of your hand in mine. __

Some things stay the same, like how we get a - long just fine. Like an

old stone wall that -'ll nev - er fall, some things are al - ways true! __

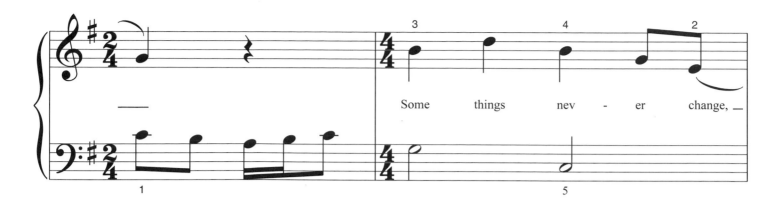

Some things nev - er change, ___

___ like how I'm hold-ing on tight to you. ELSA: Hold-ing on tight to...

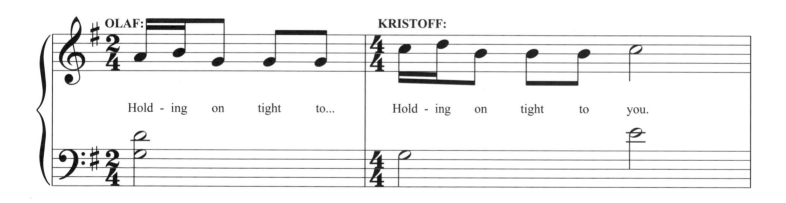

OLAF: Hold - ing on tight to... KRISTOFF: Hold - ing on tight to you.

ANNA: I'm hold-ing on tight to you.

INTO THE UNKNOWN

Music and Lyrics by KRISTEN ANDERSON-LOPEZ
and ROBERT LOPEZ

(Ah.) _____ I can

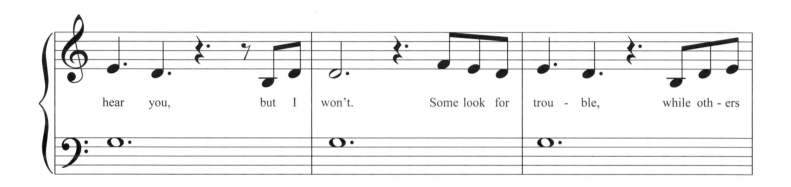

hear you, but I won't. Some look for trou - ble, while oth - ers

don't. There's a thou - sand rea - sons I should

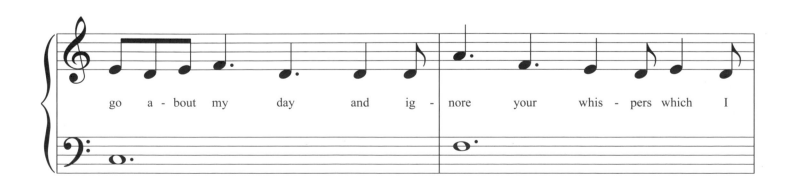

go a - bout my day and ig - nore your whis - pers which I

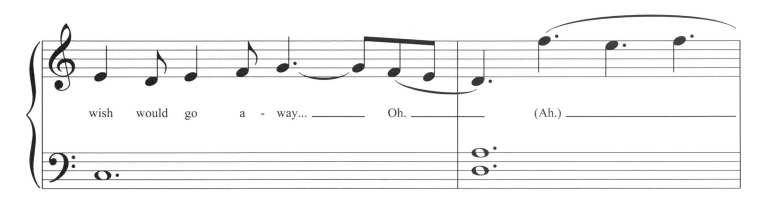

wish would go a - way... _____ Oh. _____ (Ah.) _____

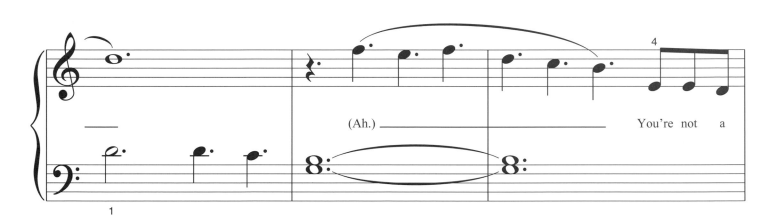

_____ (Ah.) _____ You're not a

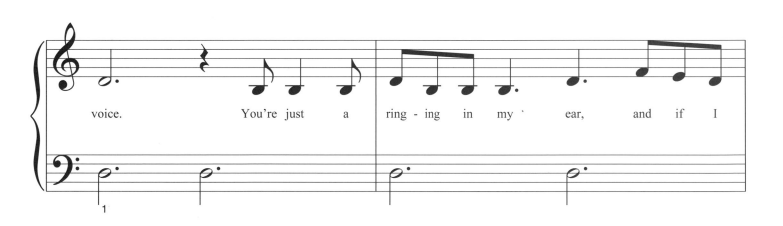

voice. You're just a ring - ing in my ' ear, and if I

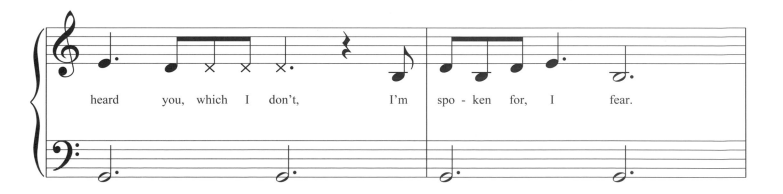

heard you, which I don't, I'm spo - ken for, I fear.

Ev - 'ry - one I've ev - er loved is here with - in these walls. ___ I'm

sor - ry, se - cret si - ren, but I'm block - ing out your calls. I've

had my ad - ven - ture. I don't need some - thing new! I'm a -

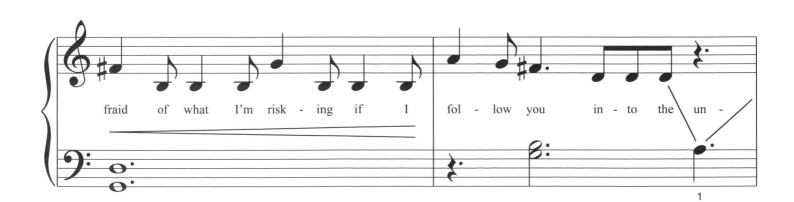

fraid of what I'm risk - ing if I fol - low you in - to the un -

known... _____ in - to the un - known... _____

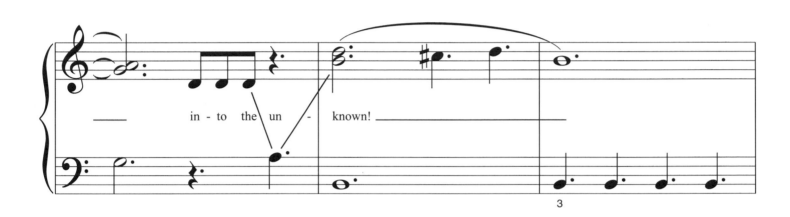

_____ in - to the un - known! _____

3

(Ah. _____) Ah.) _____

_____ In - to the un - known.

WHEN I AM OLDER

Music and Lyrics by KRISTEN ANDERSON-LOPEZ
and ROBERT LOPEZ

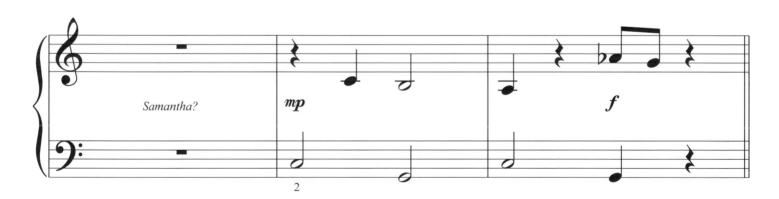

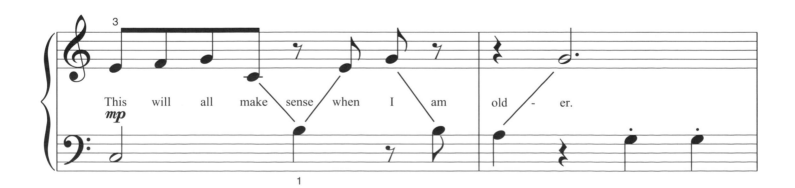

This will all make sense when I am old - er.

Some - day, I will see that this makes sense.

One day, when I'm old and wise, I'll think back and re - al - ize that

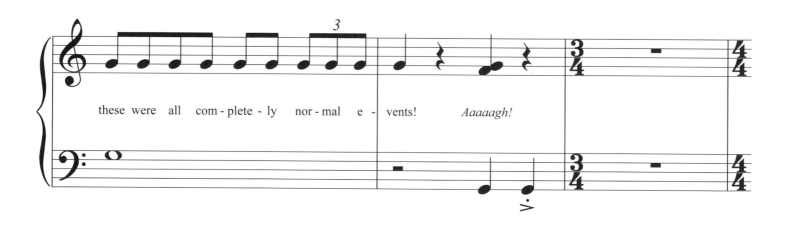

these were all com - plete - ly nor - mal e - vents! *Aaaaagh!*

I'll have all the an - swers when I'm old - er! Like,

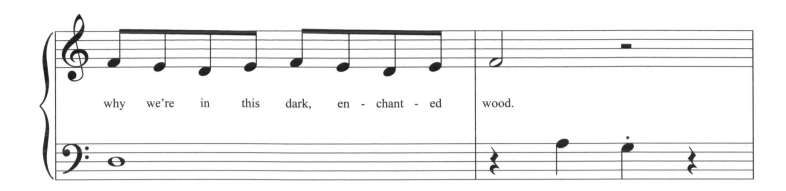

why we're in this dark, en - chant - ed wood.

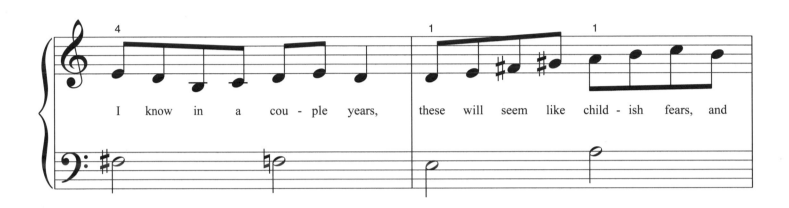

I know in a cou - ple years, these will seem like child - ish fears, and

so I know, this is - n't bad, it's good! *(Spoken:) Excuse me.* Grow - ing up means a -

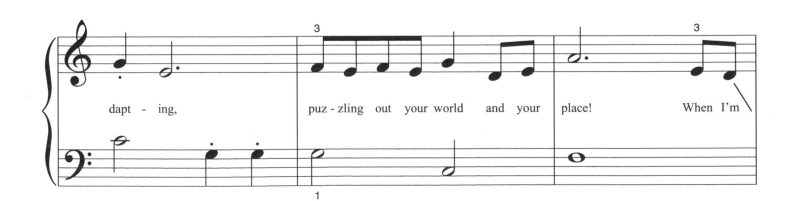

dapt - ing, puz - zling out your world and your place! When I'm

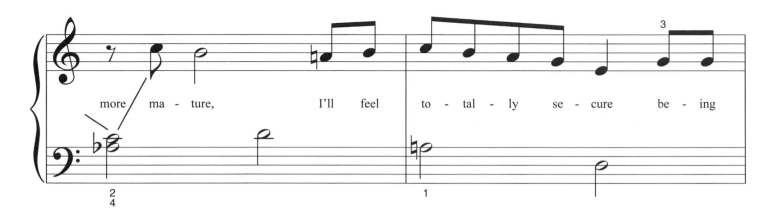

more / ma - ture, I'll feel to - tal - ly se - cure be - ing

watched by some-thing with a creep - y, creep - y face. AAAAH!!! AAAAH!!!

See, that will all make sense when I am

old - er, so there's no need to be ter - ri - fied or

Slower

tense. I'll just dream a - bout a time

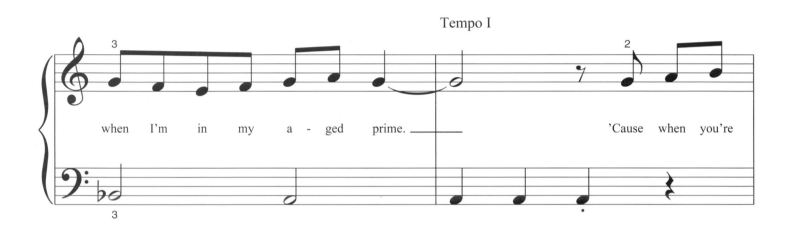

Tempo I

when I'm in my a - ged prime. 'Cause when you're

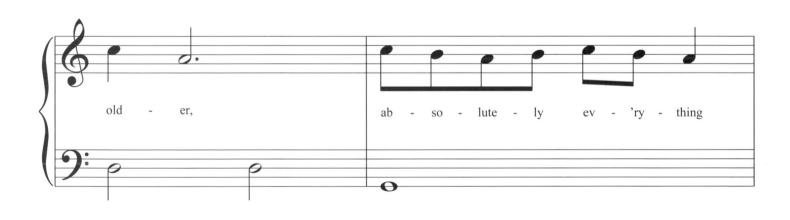

old - er, ab - so - lute - ly ev - 'ry - thing

makes sense!

REINDEER(S) ARE BETTER THAN PEOPLE (CONT.)

Music and Lyrics by KRISTEN ANDERSON-LOPEZ
and ROBERT LOPEZ

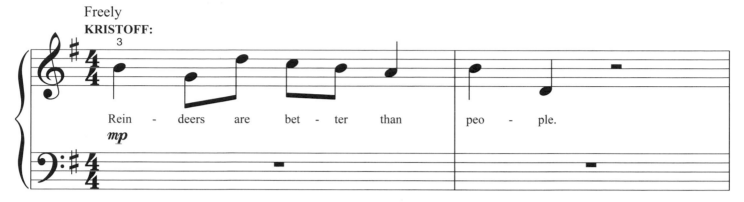

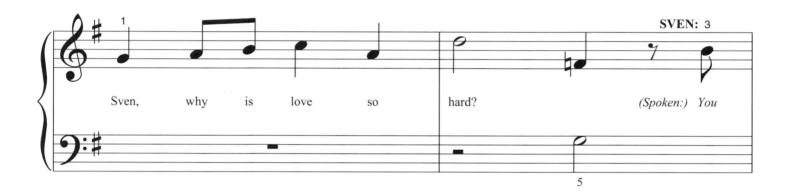

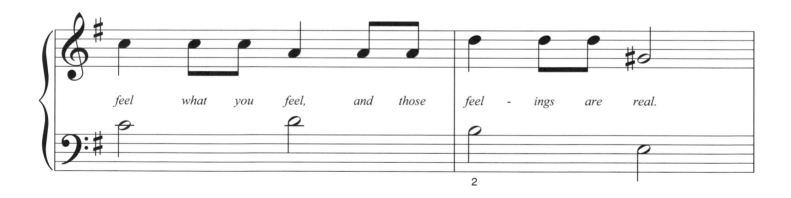

LOST IN THE WOODS

Music and Lyrics by KRISTEN ANDERSON-LOPEZ
and ROBERT LOPEZ

Moderately, in 2

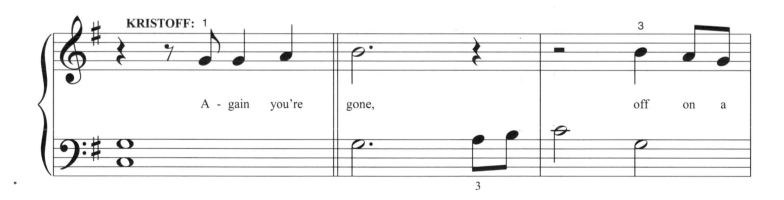

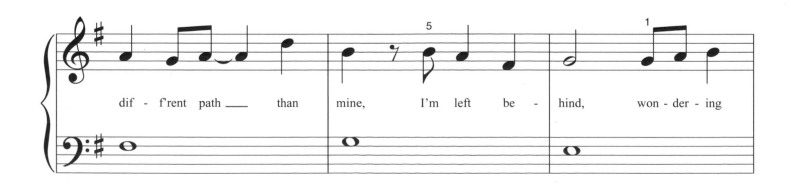

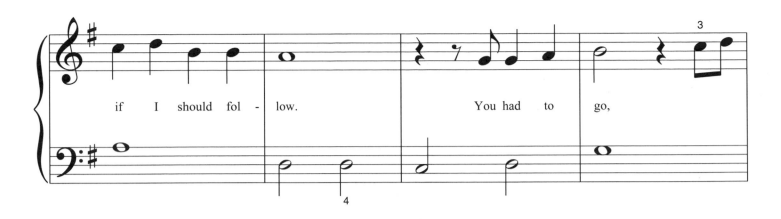

if I should fol - low.　　　　You had to go,

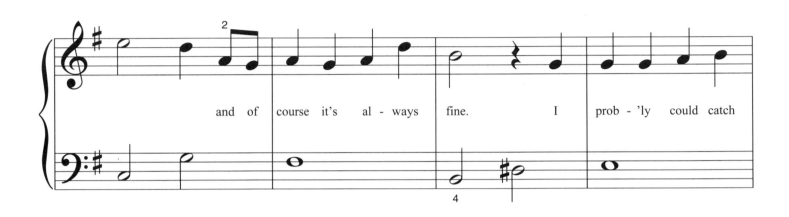

and of course it's al - ways fine.　I　prob - 'ly could catch

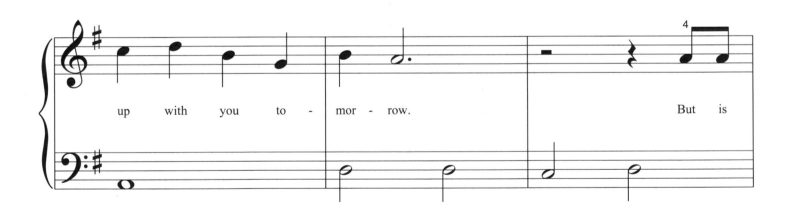

up with you to - mor - row.　　　　　　But is

this what it feels ___ like to be grow - ing a - part? ___

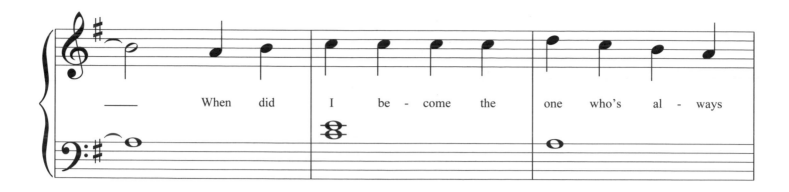

When did I be - come the one who's al - ways

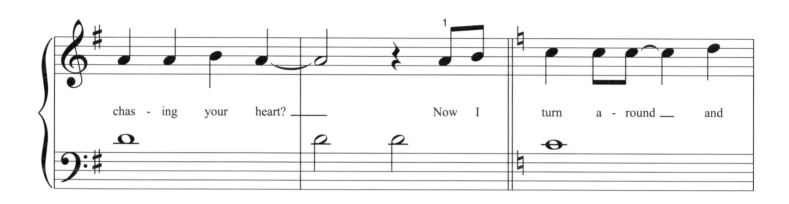

chas - ing your heart? Now I turn a - round and

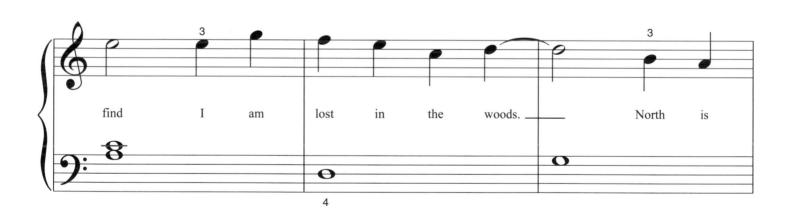

find I am lost in the woods. North is

south, right is left when you're gone. I'm the one

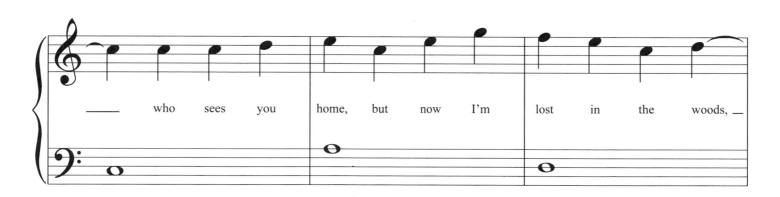

who sees you home, but now I'm lost in the woods, ___

___ and I don't know what path you are on.

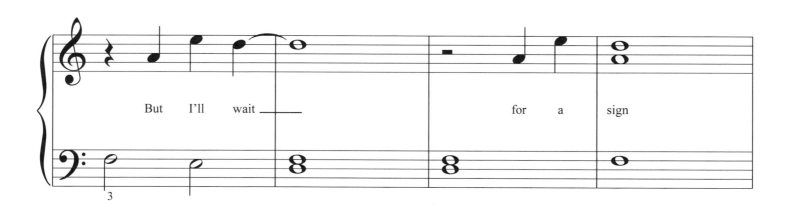

But I'll wait ___ for a sign

that I'm your path, 'cause you are mine.

Un - til   then,   I'm   lost   in   the   woods.

I'm   lost   in   the   woods.

I'm

lost   in   the   woods.

THE NEXT RIGHT THING

Music and Lyrics by KRISTEN ANDERSON-LOPEZ
and ROBERT LOPEZ

Moderately slow, with freedom

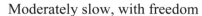

I've seen dark be-fore, but not like

this; this is cold, this is emp-ty, this is numb. The

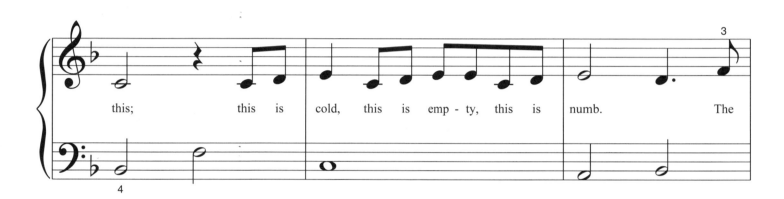

life I knew is o-ver; the lights are out. Hel-lo dark-ness, I'm read-y to suc-

cumb. I fol-low you a-round, I al-ways have, but you've

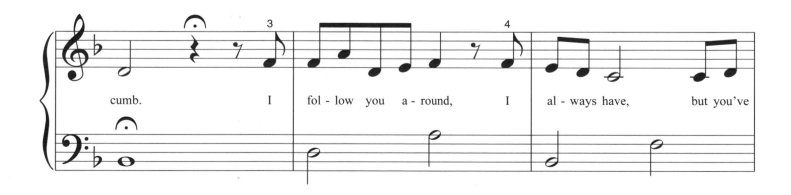

gone to a place I can - not find. This grief has a

grav - i - ty; it pulls me down. But a

ti - ny voice whis - pers in my _____ mind:

"You are lost, hope is gone, but you

must go on and do the next right

Steadily

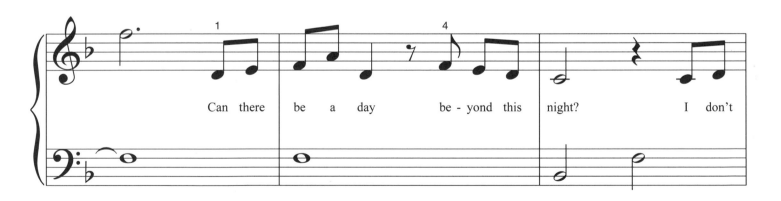

thing."

Can there be a day be - yond this night? I don't

know an - y - more what is true. I can't find my di - rec - tion; I'm

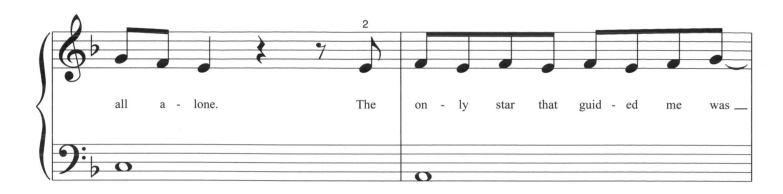

all a - lone. The on - ly star that guid - ed me was

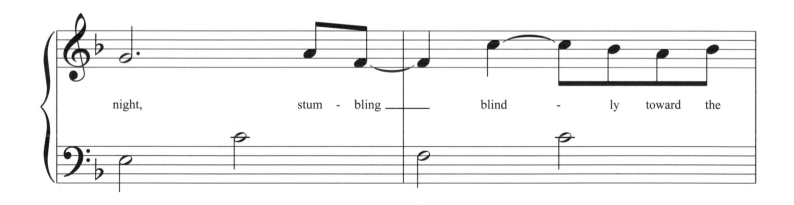

you. So I'll walk through this

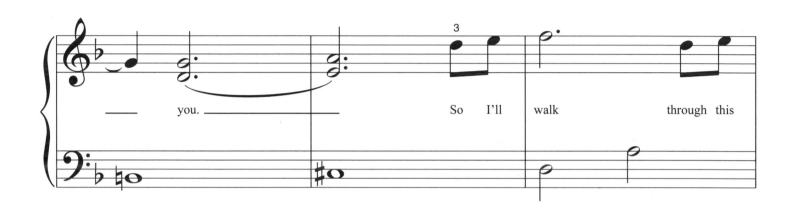

night, stum - bling blind - ly toward the

light, and do the next right thing.

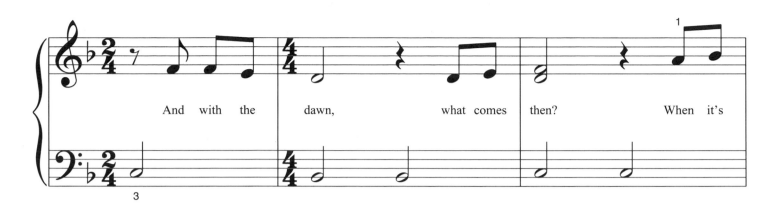

And with the dawn, what comes then? When it's

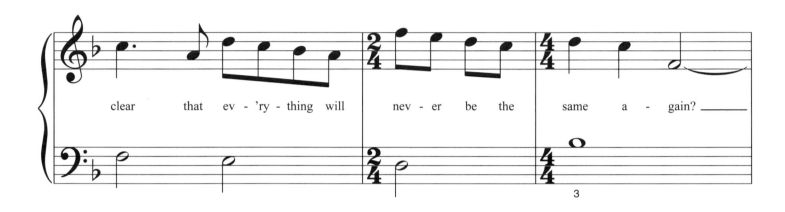

clear that ev - 'ry - thing will nev - er be the same a - gain? _____

_____ Then I'll make the choice to hear that voice, and

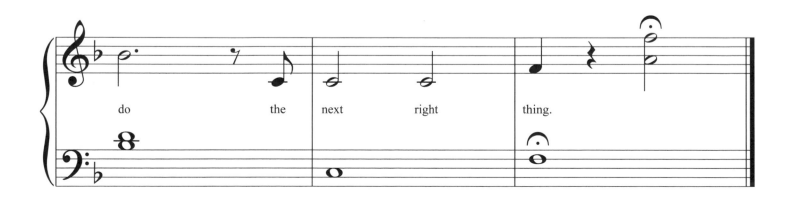

do the next right thing.

SHOW YOURSELF

Music and Lyrics by KRISTEN ANDERSON-LOPEZ
and ROBERT LOPEZ

Moving

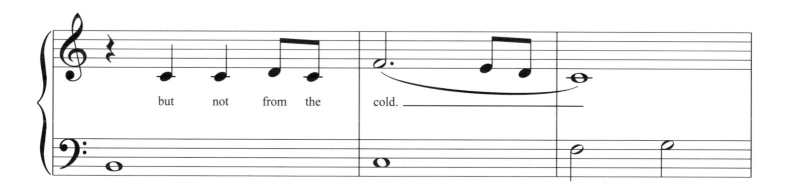

Ev - 'ry inch of me is trem - bling,

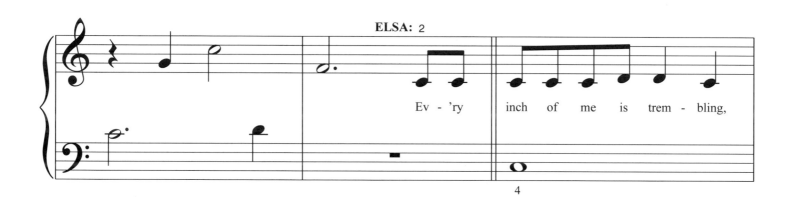

but not from the cold. _____

Some-thing is fa - mil - iar, like a dream I can reach but not quite _____

hold. I can sense you there, like a friend I've

al - ways known. _____ I'm ar - riv - ing,

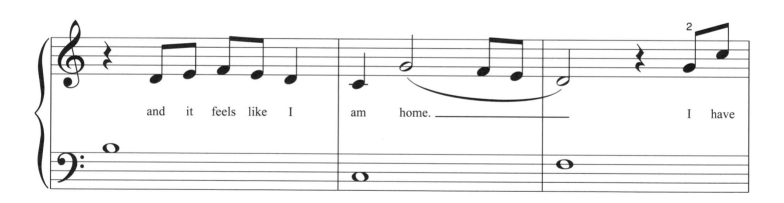

and it feels like I am home. _____ I have

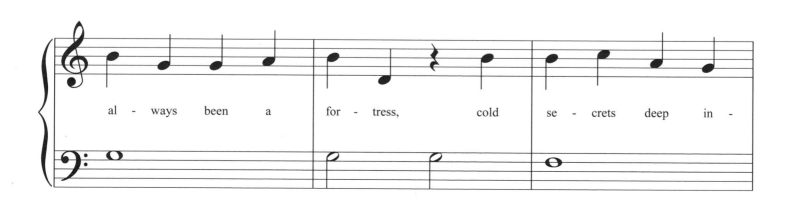

al - ways been a for - tress, cold se - crets deep in -

side. You have se - crets too, but

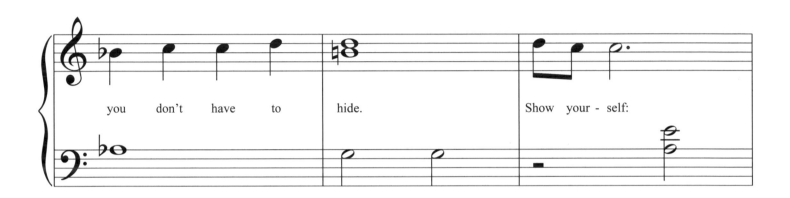

you don't have to hide. Show your - self:

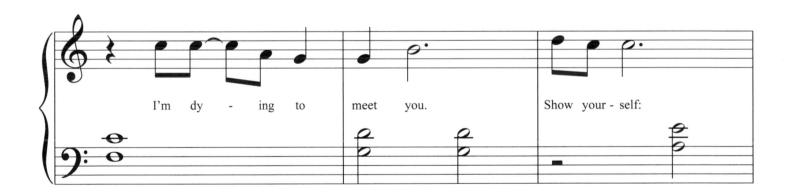

I'm dy - ing to meet you. Show your - self:

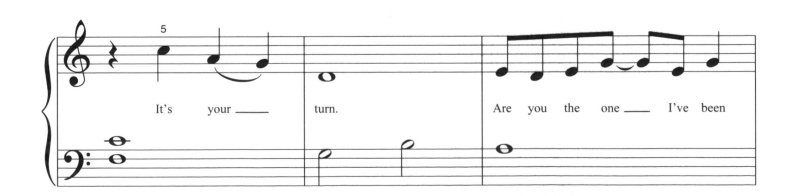

It's your _____ turn. Are you the one _____ I've been

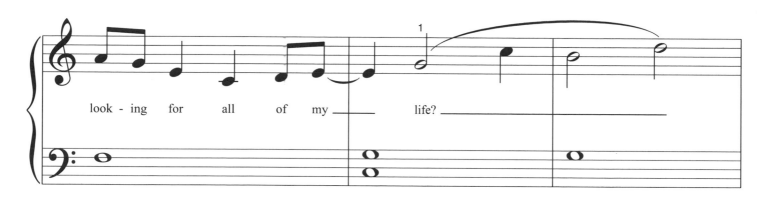

look - ing for all of my ____ life? ____

Show your - self: ____ I'm read - y to learn.

3

Ah, ____ ah. ____ Ah, ____ ah. ____

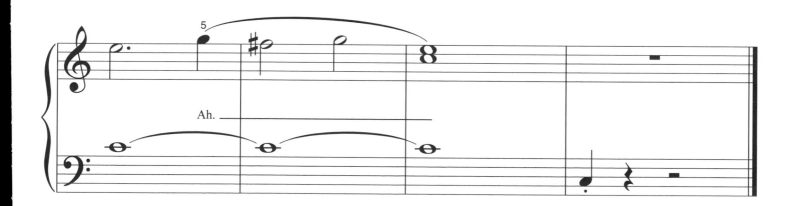

Ah. ____